tempo by angus wilson

contents

tempo · tempo · tempo · tempo · tempo · tempo · tempo · tempo · tempo · tem the impact of television on the arts

angus wilson

tempo · tempo · tempo · tempo · tempo · tempo · tempo · tempo · tempo · tempo

studio vista

Those appearing in TEMPO introduced by the Earl of Harewood, Clive Goodwin, Leonard Maguire and David Mahlowe include:

Larry Adler, Maria Albaicin, Kingsley Amis, Dominic Behan, Professor Isaiah Berlin, Robert Bolt, Peter Brook, Oscar Brown, Pamela Brown, Brenda Bruce, Baroness Budberg, Truman Capote, Lord David Cecil, Montgomery Clift, Gordon Craig, Zbigniew Cybulski, C. Day Lewis, Eithne Dunne, Michael Flanders, Ian Fleming, Juliette Greco, Sir Tyrone Guthrie, Laszlo Heltay, Donald Houston, Trevor Howard, John Huston, Eugene Istomin, Kumari Kamala, Elia Kazan, Sean Kenny, John Lanchberry, Jacques Lecoq, Professor C. S. Lewis, Joan Littlewood, Kenneth Macmillan, Marcel Marceau, Brownie McGhee, Leo McKern, Yehudi Menuhin, Jonathan Miller, Norman Morrice, Odetta, Sir Laurence Olivier, John Osborne, Donald Pleasence, Sir Herbert Read, Vanessa Redgrave, Amalia Rodrigues, Paul Rogers, Leonard Rose, Annie Ross, Anna Russell, Françoise Sagan, Pete Seeger, Segovia, Peter Sellers, Simone Signoret, Sir Basil Spence, Isaac Stern, John Stride, Graham Sutherland, Sonny Terry, Gwyn Thomas, Michael Tippett, Sophie Tucker, Kenneth Tynan, Robert Urquhart, Dame Ninette de Valois, Vicky, John Wain, Eli Wallach, Sam Wanamaker, Auberon Waugh, Western Theatre Ballet Company, Marion Williams, Richard Williams, Franco Zeffirelli.

Production staff, September 1961 to October 1964:

EXECUTIVE PRODUCER: Lloyd Shirley
PRODUCER: Reginald Collin
EDITORS: Kenneth Tynan, Peter Luke, Peter Brinson, Joan Rodker, Clive Goodwin, John Kershaw
DIRECTORS: Joe McGrath, Pamela Lonsdale, Helen Standage, Laurence Bourne, Peter Newington, Jeremy Summers, Douglas Hickox, John McGrath, Frederic Goode
DESIGNERS: Timothy O'Brien, Robert Fuest, James Goddard Voytek, Pat Downing, Terry Green

Photographs by:

Henri Cartier-Bresson (Magnum), Mark Gerson, John Timbers, The Hatton Photographic Organisation

Designed by Gillian Greenwood
© Headway Publications Limited 1964
First published by Studio Vista Limited
Blue Star House, Highgate Hill, London N19
Set in 12pt Century, 4pts leaded
Printed in Great Britain by Robert MacLehose

BARRY FOSTER
. . . more decorative than
anything

I once had the following conversation with a village shopkeeper. Shop-keeper: (in very tragic tones) Mrs Brown's dying. Me: After all she's well over ninety and she's been dying for years. She: Ah, yes, but especially lately. The arts in England, if we are to believe all we read and hear, have been especially dying lately.

I don't myself believe it. The arts seem to me to be in somewhat the same rather exciting and hopeful state of flourishing neglect by public patrons and government alike, that I remember for the last thirty years. Indeed as with most chronic invalids, there is always one branch of the arts that is making a surprising recovery. So it is now, for, if poetry is moribund, the novel shaky, theatre and music propped up only by subsidy's crutches, painting, as we all know, has found a fresh lease of life thanks to the new investment treatment.

Nevertheless in a society where growing affluence is the distinguishing feature of life, artists (except for some painters) share with the old and the widowed an embarrassing tendency to remain poor. Gone are the days when Bernard Shaw occupied a Beatle prominence in those popular newspapers which allocate celebrity space according to earning capacity. Unlike old people and widows, however, the plight of the artist in England has become a well known conversational gambit. What the arts do not receive in financial support they at least get in commiserating mention — usually by the very sort of people who in other European countries would read books or go to theatres and art galleries or attend concerts. This commiserating English public however has no intention of doing these things, so they have to find some scapegoats for their neglect of the arts. The usual cliché is to say that it's all the fault of television.

To its infamous destruction of the nation's moral fibre and its sinister incitement of British youth to violence, television, it seems, must also

FRANCO ZEFFIRELLI
Othello, the tragedy of all V.I.P.'s

add responsibility for the smug, philistinism of the mass of the English public of all classes. Television's real crime, of course, for most of these critics is that such a lot of people enjoy viewing.

If, in fact, any generalisation about the effects of television is possible, it must surely be that millions more people in this country have become familiar with the arts (if only to be given the chance to reject them) than have ever been wooed away from them. Television plays, serialisation of novels, occasional concerts, or talks on painting must at the very least have converted some thousands previously living in unregenerate ignorance — not all viewers switch off immediately they see the unfamiliar. But, oppressed perhaps by being made the scapegoat for arts' decline, television planners have tried to do more — they have organised programmes solely concerned with presenting the arts and artists to the public. Prominent among these has been *Tempo*. The present volume illustrating the highlights of *Tempo* programmes seems a suitable place to inquire what television can do to foster pleasure in music, painting, poetry, drama, ballet and architecture. And, quite as important, what have the arts as a subject matter to offer to television producers that will allow them to use the medium in new, exciting and pleasurable ways. Perhaps the successes and failures of such a programme as *Tempo* may even throw some light on whether television, apart from fostering other arts, has any creative originality to offer, is not in short only a medium but itself an art.

To many readers this may seem an unimportant question. Television brings them the plays and serials and variety they ask for and that is enough. Others will claim quite justly that television has revolutionised journalism, has added a whole dimension to documentary and, by bringing popular sociology into the home, introduced the British public to itself. This is quite true and by itself it is sufficient to give television a justification over and above its immediate powers of entertainment. But to recruit not only intelligent but sensitive and imaginative people to work for television, more is demanded. Ultimately such recruits will want to feel that television can create new forms, make statements in ways that no other medium can. And if the imagination of the British public is to keep pace with its growing education and knowledge — something that seems to me vital to our society — they are quite right: all the potentialities of television to become an independent creative art must be explored. *Tempo* has made some of the most interesting of such explorations that I have seen — not least because the producers, in largely foregoing, for various reasons, the use of cinema, have confined themselves to the scope of the television camera. Only by such disciplines can we ever know whether television has anything to offer which is not a mish-mash of cinema, theatre and magic lantern.

What emerges, I think, is exciting. *Tempo* is always at its best when exploring the processes of creation, finding out exactly how a new production of a play comes into being, how a ballet is imagined and set going, how a choir is brought into unity and so on. It is least successful when it offers us the straight performance of some musician or actor as though we were confronting them in the theatre or concert hall.

The finished work of art seems if anything diminished, certainly made flat by presentation on the telescreen; the mechanisms, the assembling of the pieces, even when the process is a familiar one like the rehearsal of a play, acquire a new and detailed significance as the camera plays upon them. It is in fact by examining the act of creation that television most successfully exalts the finished work of art; it is also in probing and presenting the creative imagination at work that the television producer seems to come nearest to producing something original of his own, a work of art. With varying degrees of success between these two extremes of ends and means *Tempo* has used its television cameras to throw all sorts of new lights upon finished works of art, even more upon the personalities of great performers and the means they use to project themselves (but then this too is in another way an exploration of the process of creation).

Of all *Tempo* programmes 'The Bundle' seems to me the most suggestive and the most visually exciting. The subject like all worthwhile themes in art is beset with dangers. To show the liberation of secondary modern school children through classes in dramatic self-expression! — the very words as I write them seem to bristle with potential sentimentality, folksiness or moral priggishness. *Tempo* entirely avoids all these. Indeed it was only when I reflected upon what might have gone wrong with such a programme — the exploitation of child photography, the homilies upon the training of the young mind, the whimsical patronage of its subject — that I even realised what horrors I had escaped, so completely were they absent from 'The Bundle'.

The programme opens with a group of boys (twelve or thirteen years old) on what seems to be wasteland beside a footpath along which adults pass by unnoticed. The boys engage in a free for all or 'bundle', beginning in ballet-like slow motion (giving that strange sense of an aquarium tank as bodies, heads, legs, arms all swim up and down the screen) the film is speeded up until the fight is fast and furious. Above this fight-dance sequence we hear the words of an authentic small boy's poem, a prize-winning entry in the competition of a national daily newspaper. 'A strange place, a place unknown, only a stone's throw from the Human Race. . . . This place you shall never find for it is mine and mine alone, strangest of all no place is so unknown'.

Visually this prelude is as mysterious as it is delightful to watch, the

strange place
place unknown . . .
he Bundle' — an exploration of children's imagination

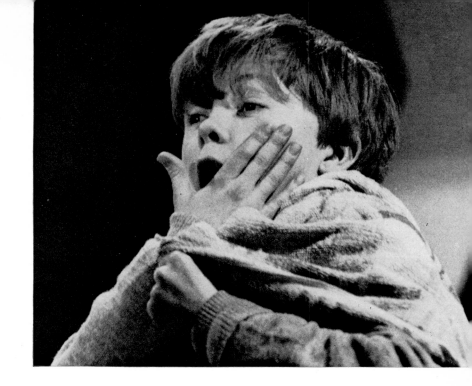

poem's words add to the mystery a sense of some private ritual invaded — as all our knowledge of children must be an invasion either of their close-kept secret society or of our own memories equally sealed by unspoken secret oath. But apart from the powerful effect of the scene and words, this prelude gives an ambiguity to the whole programme that follows which (whether intended by the producers or not) adds a whole dimension of meaning to what would otherwise be a first-rate piece of social documentary but perhaps no more.

For now the camera moves to the drama — expression class at Markfield Secondary Modern School, Tottenham. The mistress is Miss Sigley and she immediately dominates the scene. Many of the best programmes in *Tempo* are dominated by a single individual in this way — Zeffirelli, Gordon Craig — but Miss Sigley is more effective than them, for not being a well known person, the force of her personality is doubled by surprising us. The boys and girls are improvising movements to a jazz tune. Some faces, especially of the girls, are a little self-conscious and genteel, but as a whole the faces and bodies of the children express satisfaction and release so that the patterns they offer us are in turn satisfactory. A negro boy's face attracts again and again, partly because in his absorption he is so completely unselfconscious, partly because (as I notice so many times in *Tempo* programmes) black faces are always pleasing on the black and white telescreen. As the children improvise, Miss Sigley moves to the rhythm, precise and jerky, her fingers snap 'flick, flick'. She is commanding and yet she is also the young games mistress that Joyce Grenfell might so well 'take off'. I imagine that Miss Sigley would laugh at any mimicry of herself but, even if she did not, one would not be embarrassed, because she is so entirely given to her job, so integrally involved as to need to wear no self-conscious sense of mission on her face. 'Make it do something', she calls to the children, 'Use it. Use the space. Dialogue mime. Fight mime.' Flick, flick go her fingers.

Now as the children's dance continues we hear her voice over the pictures, explaining the purpose of her classes. The phrases, as I have noted some of them down, have a faintly uplifting sound — 'We all start equal in drama. We're all people. Build up a visual memory that can be called upon in work. Not cissy, not art, just making life' and so on. But this 'uplift' was not apparent in the programme, I think because of the quick camera work from children to mistress and because we saw her absorbed in her job, not speaking her message. So we avoided that slight touch of selling her mission that creeps into Miss Joan Littlewood's appearances on television — yet Miss Sigley in her own field is very much a Miss Littlewood.

Now we see the children act out a supermarket scene — the shop opening, boys and girls in pairs (husband and wife) coming in as shoppers. Then they gather round the teacher to discuss what they have done — 'It needs a climax, Miss — tragedy in a supermarket — all the shelves could collapse', 'Nickin' all the beans off the shelf, Miss', and the boy who has acted a nagging husband explains that he was saying no words, 'No, Miss, I was just muttering.' Once again it is skilled camera direction that takes away any suggestion of exploiting the charm or beauty of the children. We know that this group of school-children calls forth less spiritual exhaustion, less sense of defeated hopes than would a group of middle-aged men and women making a comparable imaginative revelation. But that is all; indeed when Miss Sigley moves on to 'work out character points', one is depressed by the sad stereotypes of adult married life that the children suggest in their portrayal of the shoppers. As she talks on, once more her views are conveyed to us over the pictures of the classroom; and once again we find her 'Aggression and moodiness tend to take over as childhood goes' and her 'Self-discipline is a must' less portentous, less dictatorial than we would in an interview where the teacher is shown divorced from the scene of her work, mouthing theory into the unco-operative emptiness of the television studio.

And now we come to the culmination of the drama class — a scene in a barber's shop in which the boys *act out* the aggressions which we have seen at the beginning released in the conventional, casual, uncontrolled, street scene, 'bundle'. This barber's shop play with its rhythmic musical accompaniment and its gay, jerky movement as of some silent film comedy ends appropriately in a free for all Keystone Cops mess of lather and shaving brushes and custard-pie faces.

The aggression has been released in farce, but that it is still the same aggression we can see from the faces of the girls who watch both aghast and admiring at this scene of comic virility put on for them by the boys.

Miss Sigley's purpose is achieved, the childrens' imaginations and bodies freed, our sense of social responsibility satisfied. Or is it? For this is where the ambiguity of the opening passage makes its mark. Of the integrity and humanity of Miss Sigley's aims we can have no doubt, of the genuine imaginative impulses released in the children we can feel assured. Perhaps this is how aimless violence may be avoided. And yet this has been, for all its improvisation, an adult organised release of the child imagination. What of the small boy's poem with which we started? 'This place you shall never find for it is mine and mine alone. Strangest of all no place is so unknown.' As a citizen I admired and approved Miss Sigley's course. As a novelist, I wondered — isn't this just another benevolent editor or publisher directing the creator's images?

Whatever the answer, the programme really arouses thought about creative imagination. It works visually and aurally with the minimum of verbal interpretation and with the maximum of camera playing freely upon the free play of children. It is this technical aptitude, this verbal economy which is the most striking feature of the progress that *Tempo* programmes have made from their beginnings in 1961. Perhaps the only programme at all comparable with 'The Bundle' is an early venture called 'Mental Health' which discussed the aesthetic validity of the paintings of psychotic patients. Both subjects are on the surface sociological and therapeutic, but both in fact dig deep beneath the roots of creative imagination. The fantasies played out by the children in 'The Bundle' are not such Blakean songs of innocence that we can entirely separate them from the aggressive fantasies of some of the paintings shown in 'Mental Health'. We may prefer to side with Wordsworth against Freud, but few of us would be astonished now to find in children's games and art the seeds of the strange schizoid painting of one patient with its secret, separate castle ('This place you shall never find') or even the horrible ordered symmetry and flat patterns of the paranoid. Potentially 'Mental Health' had as much to offer although more sensationally than 'The Bundle', but it was loaded with verbal interpretation — narrator, commentator, and at last the familiar neutralising tones of expert critics as Herbert Read, Francis Haskell and Wayland Young sat before us asking, can a man be both patient and artist? The opinions were neither worse nor better than in most such discussions — 'All art is a form of escape from hell' and so on; but as that familiar sentence, 'At that point I'm afraid we must leave. . . .' sounded in my ears I rejoiced, as later when I saw 'The Bundle' come to an end I longed for more. Those two programmes on the sources of imagination are divided, I think, by a whole ocean of television imaginative production.

Having a grand time at Blackpool...

Cartier-Bresson documents the English on holida

Trevor Howard and Leo McKern

Vision of England'
mpo's homage to Shakespeare

onald Houston in the hands of the make-up artist

Pierrot, too moonstruck to shove the narrator out of camera

False premise

The American show 'The Premise' revealed its secret to *Temp*

but standing up or lying down they were equally fla

'The Scapegoat'
Lloyd Reckord and Anthony Nicholls in a programme for Easter

The guard pleads for the life of the victim

Laszlo Heltay — Hungarian conductor — shows us that 'Carols mean Christmas

Bedsitter manhood — the mask . .

'The Bundle' succeeds admirably, but it may well be objected that whether or not the paintings of psychotics can be considered art, the free expression of twelve-year-olds is no more than an improvised school play. Art, not the untutored imagination, is the subject of *Tempo*, and art is altogether more difficult than camera-trapping children, however dexterously their secret wonderings may have been caught. The objection has some force, for 'The Bundle' (though, in fact, far more) gains by its strong element of sociology; and documentary, as I have suggested, is television's one certain, overwhelming victory. What about trapping the artist, the adult sane creative imagination? Has television the art to do it?

There immediately springs to mind the *Tempo* programme — 'The Medium-Sized Cage', the story of the inventing and making of a television comment by a group of students at the Film and T.V. Design Section of the Royal College of Art. I write 'comment' for the invention was neither play nor documentary nor plain performance, it was something moving between all three, peculiarly designed by the students I suppose, to illustrate the special properties of that medium-sized cage — the television box. The title comes from Samuel Beckett's *Murphy* where it is used to describe the desolate, anonymous yet enclosing qualities of the typical bedsitting room. The programme takes us from a group of students devising the programme to the comment itself — the picture internal and external of a young man (art student — one time would be sculptor) 'moving digs'. With the background sound of a jazz group and the foreground details of empty bedsitters changing from anonymity to obsession as they fill up with the possessions (pin-ups, health and strength, comic-photo montage, ton-up equipment, skull and crossbones, science-fiction masks, and above all, shiny black leather boots) which give our hero his existence, we hear him — 'outsider', provincial, nearly twenty-four years old, everyman's Albert Finney — in interior monologue over the detailed camera work. 'Interests — sex, being alive and myself', 'War and death relate to myself', 'I wonder who lived here and collected all this junk?' 'Organs, religion, churches repel me', 'I could make some of these working class films, give me the money' — the thoughts, if now familiar, are authentic. And so he *could* make one of these working class films, but what is made in 'The Medium-Sized Cage' is the distillation of *Saturday Night and Sunday Morning* or *This Sporting Life*, reduced to this single figure and his stream of consciousness, with his every associated object lovingly caressed in turn by the television cameras. The combination discloses a whole world of lusts, fantasies, ambitions and frustrations in a single set with a single actor, by using, as only television can, voice and pictures to combine the literary techniques of the naturalist like Zola with those of Joyce. This double technique is television's greatest gift to artistic economy. Here the process can be peculiarly brief, for we know the young man's type so well before the action starts. Publicity today has already reduced him to self-parody. As he says, with the inverted commas of self-consciousness, 'My philosophy — anarchism!' So far has the outsider travestied himself since Colin Wilson first burst forth upon the English scene.

I have written that the camera dwells most lovingly upon the objects, the junk of the young man's life and sequences of his daydreams, but this is perhaps not quite accurate, for it is above all upon the young man himself as he stretches on his dreary bed — 'the boxer must have a dressing room to relax in' — that the camera descends, catching all his drifting daydreams and the self-mockery with which he protects himself from them. Each line of his body seems to suggest an aimless wandering that mocks those flashing jackboots, symbol of his cherished toughness and virility, to which the camera turns again and again in ironic comment.

There is nothing here, of course, that cinema could not do, but the mammoth scope of cinema could never content itself with caressing so limited an area of physical reality, so confined and repetitious a consciousness, nor probe so deeply, even for the short-running time of 'The Medium-Sized Cage'.

The programme ends with a return to the students telling us of their social backgrounds and ambitions. Once again this emphasis on the creators seems an intrusion on what they have created. However, at least, they are not indulging in commentary on their work; they are telling us of themselves, and their accents proudly proclaiming almost every region of Great Britain offer authenticity for the portrait of youth on the move that they have offered us. The only puzzle that remains is why students of television should produce something so exact and sufficient, and television companies produce such. . . . But there is no mystery really. One can imagine exactly the kind of overplotted, socially significant play into which this comment would be blown up by most drama departments. And one knows exactly the many spurious pressures that would make for such inflation.

With 'The Medium-Sized Cage', however, we are still with one foot in documentary, and the other foot in television itself, which, alas, is a tautology if we wish to show that television is an art. There are two immediate directions by which we can find our way out of television into older means of expression — by way of cinema or by way of theatre.

Tempo has largely avoided programmes about cinema (though there was at least one notable one about Polish film acting marred only by the tedium of listening to an interpreter). I am sure that this has been a wise decision. The love-hate relationship of television and cinema is demonstrated in the mixture of dependence and contempt with which television planners use old films to fill in programme gaps. The public, shrewdly as usual, exactly echoes this mood in the loving grumbling with which it greets these substituted old cinema favourites. Cinema in space and motion can do so much more than television; television, by way of revenge, seems to reduce the films it presents to a kind of animated magic lantern show. As for tracing the processes of cinema creation, these, where they are not too technical for the average viewer to follow, are too close to those of television itself. The viewer would only be presented with an enormously magnified version of that studio scenery and life which, since someone brightly thought of doing without props, has been the increasingly deadening and monotonous background to so many television programmes, from interviews to variety.

The relationship between television and live theatre is a far more subtle one and *Tempo* has made many attempts, some excellent, others less good, to get at some of the facts that lie behind the mystique of 'good theatre' so strongly adhered to by that intuitive profession. The least successful programmes about theatre were those which attempted to give the flavour of a current show in excerpt, such as 'Lions led by Donkeys', the programme about *Oh, What a Lovely War*. I write 'about', but this was really the trouble; I do not think that a viewer who had not seen the show on the stage would have really known from the television programme what it *was* about, except in the most general terms. The commentator kept his explanations to the minimum. In general this is the greatest virtue that a commentator can show — and even here it was not perhaps more explanation that was needed but more passion in explaining. Of course, I was at a disadvantage in knowing the stage original well, but it seemed to me that the shot of the wonderfully funny 'Roses are Blooming in Picardy' or the deeply moving Christmas 1914 in the trenches failed to convey the emotions that came off the stage. There were Murray Melvin and Victor Spinetti doing their stuff and yet somehow the life had gone from it; I could only be excited by remembering what I had felt in the theatre. There was not enough of the show, nor enough coherence in the excerpts to convey Miss Littlewood's peculiarly powerful propaganda, so powerful because of the very over-simplifying that makes it so infuriating, or her wonderful mockery of fruity music hall. A more passionate commentary might have welded it together; but the subject that demands passionate commentary is, I think, wrongly chosen for television. Which is not to say that it should not have been shown — one of television's functions is to give a taste of contemporary plays or books for those who would not otherwise see them — but only that it was good entertainment but uninteresting television.

Something of the same difficulty attended the two programmes 'Ad Absurdum' about the theatre of the absurd. Yet here the excerpts and discussions based on Martin Esslin's book had such variety of laughter and gloom that the viewer, who was not amazed and shocked by the outrageous novelty of it all (and thousands of viewers must have been), could be kept alert by the sheer jolting as he swung on the maniac-depressive pendulum from Ionesco to Beckett to Pinter to Simpson. Yet, if it had not been for the wonderful virtuoso acting of Kenneth Griffith — television more even than the stage showed what a lively actor can get in sheer liberation from talking nonsense — 'Ad Absurdum' would have primarily served to show how, if cinema evades television through movement, the theatre (particularly the verbose theatre of *Waiting for Godot*) weighs the television screen down with its static inertia. In Ionesco's famous play *Amédée* the corpse of the lover grows and grows until it fills the flat — he is suffering from 'geometrical progression — the incurable disease of the dead'. Even this slow morbid growth seems lively beside the stillness of Beckett's tramps and dustbins and rubbish heaps.

No, once again, it is the making of the play, not the play itself, that television can bring alive. With the right personality, it must at once be said. From the earliest days of *Tempo* (as one might expect with Kenneth Tynan, the original inspiration of the programme) theatrical production and acting had a front place. The first of such programmes used interviews with cut-ins of filmed live productions or of stills to illustrate theatrical reminiscence. Interview has its faults, but they are perhaps exaggerated in television circles nowadays. It is primarily on interview surely that television's brilliant journalistic achievement has been built up. The faulty development has been to overpower the personalities of the interviewed by the creation of celebrated interviewers (whether wreathed in smoke like Muggeridge or frozen into ice blocks like Freeman). The theatrical interviews on *Tempo* told me a lot about the effects of interviewing on television. The interview between Dan Farson and Gordon Craig at the old man's home in Vence was one of the most memorable I have seen on television. Farson seemed quite obliterated (as an interviewer should be) by the force of the ninety-year-old Craig's personality — so reminiscent of the Yellow Book era in his mixture of elaborate imagery ('Irving's voice was like a leopard's smile') and epigrammatic malice ('Stanislavsky's method? I don't think I really know it. He was not very serious over it, I think').

After Gordon Craig's performance, Elia Kazan's New York serious 'theatre' manner (the New York intelligentsia is often portentous, theatre people being serious are always heavy-handed, but the combination!) seemed like an embarrassingly sincere undergraduate talking his way through a tutorial for which he'd done no reading. Yet in the end I was to discover that it was not Gordon Craig's personality that made Farson's interview with him so excellent; it was rather that Farson was literally not there. He had arrived at Vence with a cold and the old man's nonagenarian caution had rightly excluded him. Recipe, then, for a really good interview. Let the interviewee talk and mix afterwards with a few shots of the interviewer.

Another personality interviewed early on (by Tynan himself and very skilfully) was Franco Zeffirelli. His mixture of overpowering boyish charm, tenacity and toughness, and his original views that hang dangerously between the sublime and the vulgar made him even in that interview, where the formidable Joan Littlewood was third party, the figure that mattered. Miss Littlewood, using all her zany little-girl tricks, tried to hammer Zeffirelli on his *Othello* production. 'First thing I'd do,' she told him, 'is clear the stage . . . make the audience work . . . cut psychology, cut character analysis.' All good straight left stuff that we have heard her dish up before. In fact, I agree with it. But it somehow seems empty when Zeffirelli (tough-charm boy any time to match Joan Littlewood's little-girl stuff) tells us that he has set out to give the 'pompous state life of Venice', to show in *Othello* 'the tragedy of all V.I.P. men'. The reasoning is good, however much it is only an excuse for the high romanticism he craves. The resulting *Othello* may veer from the highest poetic tragedy to a suggestion of what Duse would have been like produced by Tree, but in a theatre world dedicated to improvisation Zeffirelli's extravagances are intensely exciting.

It was then a spendid inspiration of the *Tempo* producers to show Zeffirelli rehearsing John Stride as Hamlet and Pamela Brown as Gertrude in the closet scene. An even better inspiration to call it 'A Wind of Change'. Zeffirelli in interview, of course, was only an hors d'oeuvre to Zeffirelli in rehearsal. The mobility of his face is of a very unusual kind. Most men with conventional good looks (and Zeffirelli is very good-looking) can look noble or sentimental as required. Zeffirelli's version of nobility is somehow savage and violent, his version of softer emotions is just on the edge of the clown. Since he mimes every gesture his actors make, the rehearsal would be a magnificent show if nothing else. But it is, in fact, much more, for Zeffirelli's method of instruction, for all his charm, is steely rather than silken. From the beginning of the act until at any rate the murder of Polonius we saw conflict in the making of art — conflict between Zeffirelli and John Stride as Hamlet — conflict in which, despite an obvious real friendliness between the two men, Stride clearly found the producer's ideas doubtful and alien to him. Zeffirelli made it clear that what *he* thought was 'what happened in Hamlet'. He posited at least three unorthodox views. Hamlet, when he kills Polonius, is relieved for he believes that he has killed the King and solved his dilemma; Hamlet hated his father who had sent him to Wittenburg because he did not think him a suitable heir to the throne; no ghost appears in the closet scene. Of these three propositions Stride sensibly seized on the second, for it is certainly the most outrageous. But Zeffirelli, for all his limited command of English and his boyish manner, won the day by aggression, determination and belief in himself. The film of the Italian production of *Hamlet* that followed seemed a slight anticlimax. It was a relief to see giant romantic acting again — Gordon Craig would have loved it. But the really exciting moment had been the conflict that went into its making — the short, fierce clash of wills between producer and actor. And its resolution in Zeffirelli's favour. Too often on television the arts appear to be all sweetness and light, but art is founded on conflict and tension, and for a moment we had seen the very core of creative conflict in action.

'Stanislavsky's method?
Not very serious, I think'
Gordon Craig

Truman Capote and Kenneth Tynan
elegance before ea

Do it yoursel
Donald Pleasance, television actor of the year 196
makes up for Anouilh's '*Poor Bitos*' in 'A Dialogue of Actor

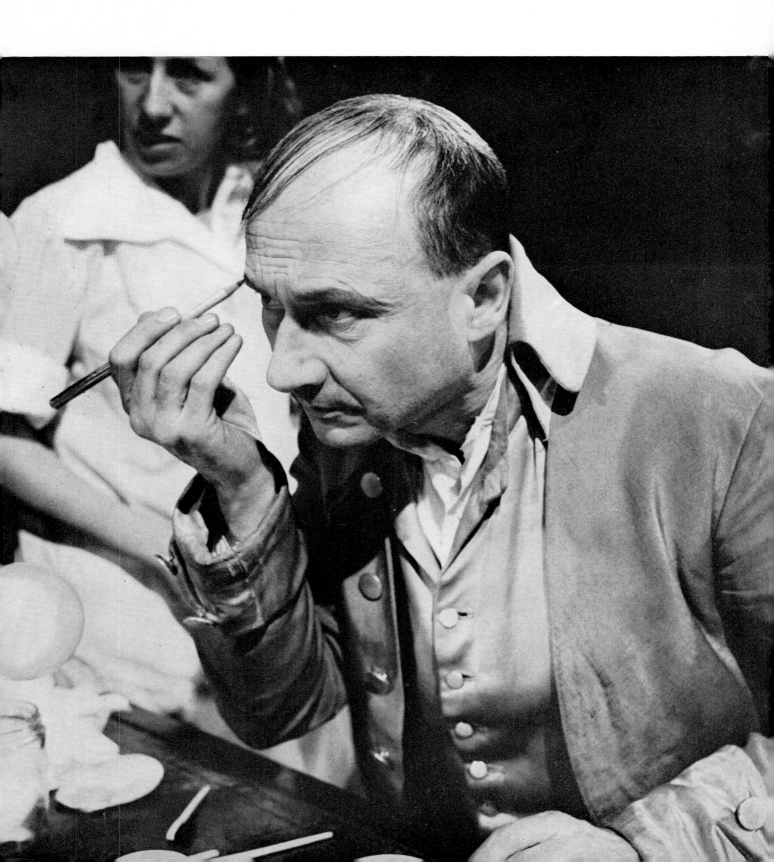

The happiest days of her life?
Brenda Bruce in Beckett's *Happy Days*

'...eometrical Progression —
...e incurable disease of the dead. . . .'
...ter Duguid and Gretchen Franklin in Ionesco's *Amédée*

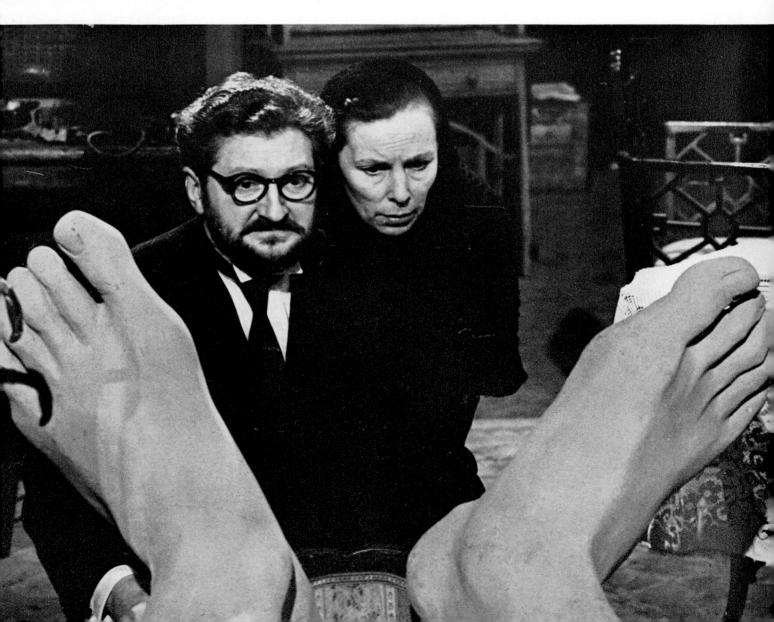

Zeffirelli in 'A Wind of Change'
rehearsals of Pamela Brown and John Stride in *Hamlet*

Alas, he's mad. . . .'

'*Si t'imagines* . . .
Juliette Greco

the act and the movement

So far we have talked about creative art and its sources, but *Tempo* has, of course, been as much concerned with interpretative artists as with those who create. For a large part of its audience, I suspect, these star artists will be the greatest attraction of the programmes. Indeed a programme of the *Tempo* kind, at present, often fulfils a special function in offering full-length performances by artistes like Juliette Greco, Amalie Rodrigues, Oscar Brown, or even more 'popular' singers like Annie Ross — artistes outside the strict line of popular entertainment that regulates the choice of 'variety' on television. This is a valuable function of a programme like *Tempo* even within the strictest terms of its role of presenting the arts, for viewers are given a chance to extend the range of their taste, to see new trends or techniques, and above all, to break down that wretched barrier between entertainment and art which would divide the world into self-satisfied philistines and self-congratulating prigs.

The problem for the television producer in showing interpreters (singers, dancers, instrumentalists) seems to me quite different to anything we have considered in the first two sections. A short examination of the programme 'A World Full of Grey' presenting Oscar Brown may show what I mean: Mr Brown as a negro, shared with another programme 'God's Trombones' which featured the cast of *Black Nativity* the peculiar advantage of giving a special value to black and white photography. Mr Brown is in fact at the opposite pole to the cast of *Black Nativity* both in movement (the visual essence of such interpretative programmes) and in message though both are propagandist entertainers. Nevertheless to see the lithe black panther-like grace of Oscar Brown or the solid ebony majesty of the contralto soloist of *Black Nativity* is immediately to realise that this is black and white photography needed for its own sake, and that all the rest of the time we are forgetting what is only a convention imposed by necessity.

Oscar Brown then starts with the fullest advantages of movement and colour. His repertory is intended to take the negro spiritual away from submission (away even from the dignified, primitive Christian submission of *Black Nativity*) to the new mood of racial anger and social protest to which the American negro community is now awakening. He echoes the voice of James Baldwin, the total rejection of all folksiness, charm, childlikeness or any other supposed negro quality which whites have found it easy to patronise. Sometimes his songs appeared to conform to all that the whites have cosily expected from the negroes and then at an unexpected moment they lash out in biting fury; sometimes his songs maintained a hot anger throughout. The programme had a short introduction by a compère, though with songs so direct and violent as Mr Brown's it seems unlikely that any viewer capable of seeing the screen and hearing the words could miss what he intended to communicate. Indeed the simplicity of his fierceness is his third great advantage, for in a short programme the immediacy of a message makes its strongest impact — there may be angry rejection, but there is no time for reasoned dispute. Along with the immediacy, the lack of subtlety in Mr Brown's message goes a corresponding clarity of performance: he is an essentially dramatic singer whose every movement and expression are definite and on the attack. The only ambiguity in his personality is the co-existence of great anger and high gaiety, and this, as we soon realise, is a product of his assurance, the new assurance of his race. They can afford to be gay in the midst of their anger because victory is with them — they can afford, as Mr Brown sometimes does, to clown in their anger. They can afford to . . . but does it succeed? Does Oscar Brown succeed? I think this question has to be asked and juxtaposed to the ambition and assurance of his message. Only a minority of viewers will be wholeheartedly with him — if, that is, they have really understood what he is saying. This is not a popular or comfortable thing to write because to deny majority support for the negro cause seems like letting it down. But I do believe that in the uncompromising form in which Oscar Brown and other negro leaders rightly pose their claims the negro programme will just not come home to most white people, even in a country so far from the centre of the battle as England. They have been used to too many centuries of belief in their superiority to *understand* that they are no longer being asked for sympathy (this the better white people have found easy for a long time), no, they are being told what negro people intend to do with their own lives. To get that simple message over to English viewers without being met by a self-protective incomprehension demands a great range of talents from the performer. These, I think, Oscar Brown mainly has.

In the first place he is so evidently carried away by his own message that there can be no feeling that he is 'putting something over'. And yet he is so palpably a conscious, highly aware artist, that there is no chance of patronising him as a primitive, a 'natural'. Then he arranges his repertory in an order of attack upon his audience that is like some beautifully organised speech. First a direct and dramatic appeal to decency and a summoning up of all the historical injustice that negroes have suffered in the States — the sale of a young slave girl (grand-daughter of an African queen). We are brought slap into our memories of Uncle Tom and all the emotions that his name still arouses. Then an appeal to the ordinariness in viewers, the 'get together' approach in 'a fellow I know folks call Sam. . . .' ending 'I believe in Sam'. There is for me a certain touch of patronage in anything that sets out to describe 'the ordinary fellow' but Oscar Brown almost gets away with it. Now with 'Forty Acres and A Mule' he feels ready to break through the image of the patient, decent negro beloved by white liberals. 'An urgency of patience held too long', he tells us, and 'I am being rowdy hot and black'. Then, pushing the attack, he points to the new Africa from which the American negro draws his new sence of urgency and assurance — 'Afroblue'. Then he takes the old maxims that the 'wise' negroes had learned through 'the discipline of restraint of centuries of slavery'; for example, 'Whatever happens don't blow your cool'. He rends them to pieces with his anger and points the way to a new burning heat.

So far, so very good — if viewers haven't exactly got what he means, they'll at least know that he *means* it and that it isn't at all comfortable, for all the gaiety and high spirits with which it has been put across. He successfully combines entertainment with propaganda (or uplift); and this is no mean feat, for from the earliest days of music hall there has seldom been anything more embarrassing than the sudden serious 'turn' (religious, patriotic, or folksy moralising) of the good comic entertainer. Oscar Brown banishes this embarrassment at one blow by so totally fusing his serious message, his propaganda with his 'act', fusing the two by the emotional passion which seems to dominate even the most lighthearted, clowning side of his personality. But for me the beautifully constructed repertory, the oratory, was robbed of some of its persuasion by its peroration — his last song — 'Brown Baby'. It is not so much that the song has a too easy sentimentalism, though I think it has, nor that it moralises in too hackneyed words, though it does, but that these words, 'Our world too is full of grey' and 'I want you to live by the justice order, I want you to walk down the freedom road' seemed suddenly to relax his fierce attack, to make an appeal

'I believe in Sam.

Marion Williams

directly to his viewers that is not in keeping with his previous fierce-funny calculated aggression. For the first time I found myself yearning for Bessie Smith — and when a white viewer starts yearning for Bessie Smith, it is a certain sign that he is longing for the tragedy and pathos that were so essential a part of the negro life before the new militancy was born. Perhaps it was the success of Mr Brown's attack that made me hurry back to my memories of that great tragic singer who was so unpolitical, but I think it was because he didn't carry me with him in his last song. In fairness I must say, however, that striking and often moving though the singers of *Black Nativity* were, their simple religious propaganda made me long for Bessie Smith all the time as an antidote, whereas Oscar Brown's social militancy held me almost to the end.

It will be clear that a programme like 'A World Full of Grey' demands far more direct comment on its content and far less on its television presentation. By and large the producers seem to have done their job when in selecting Oscar Brown, they realised his visual and aural potentiality on the screen. For the rest the cameras may work against his effects by obtrusive cleverness that interferes with the lines of his telling movements. *Tempo* cameras behaved with admirable discretion it seemed to me, but *Tempo* designers with rather less, placing him either in a too consciously dramatic blaze of light or against a vague backcloth which nevertheless suggested the late C. B. Cochran and showbiz.

This question of backcloth or design is never, I think, more important than when, as with solo performers, it seems least obtrusive. The failure of Segovia's appearance in one of the programmes was made worse by the stage upon which he was set — a platform that seemed like something arranged for a mannequin display at a leading London

department store. It is not an easy matter, for a touch of glitter suggests
showbiz and Bandwagon, decor too often recalls 'The Black and White
Minstrels', the studio in all its camera nakedness has become a mad-
dening cliché, and even attempted realism may misfire, as I found when
criticising a terrible picture-window behind Yehudi Menuhin's rehearsal, only to be told that it was an exact reproduction of the picture-
window in his home. But that it should be given the most exact atten-
tion when a stage-type performance is being shown I have no doubt, for
even the most brilliant performance can be marred by a background
that unluckily suggests some conflicting stereotype.

Interpretative art of the near-cabaret sort proved highly successful
in the *Tempo* programmes, but the same cannot be said of more classical
performers. The static figure of Segovia proved once again that no
close-ups of a guitarist's fingerwork, let alone of his irrelevant knees
or boots can do more than intolerably distract from the music he plays.
Segovia, poor man, suffered more than most from narrator commentary
(that bugbear of early *Tempo* which is now almost gone) 'You can really
hear the soul of Spain' is not the sort of comment that one wishes to
hear. A more hopeful approach to serious music might seem, as with
the theatre, to be in the analysis of a rehearsal. I still believe that this
might be successful, even after seeing the programme of Menuhin and
his fellow performers practising the Mozart clarinet quintet. What we
saw, in fact, did not seem to be a rehearsal, but a play through of the
work, with a little desultory chatter and some programme notes (surely
not at all what the professional musicians would want or need to hear)
provided from time to time by Menuhin. The truth is that, whereas
Zeffirelli set his rehearsal in a blaze by his personality, Menuhin
merely damped his down by his domination.

Classical music, then, whether in direct performance or in rehearsal, has not so far been elucidated by *Tempo*. Even Laszlo Heltay's personality could not fire the rehearsal of the Collegium Musicum Oxoniense. They seemed like hearty, music-loving young men and women in a hundred choirs in England, singing Wássail when they were told to sing Wassáil; nor did the cameras help by picking out irrelevant details of the medieval decoration in the hall of Merton College.

But ballet proved, I thought, quite successful in the performance of 'Mods and Rockers' by the Western Theatre Ballet, and triumphant in the analysis of creation with the programme 'The Choreography of Norman Morrice'. I except the 'Mods and Rockers' performance from full praise because it was marred by a pretentious and unnecessary sociological commentary by Mike Sarne. Authorities on teenagers have a special smugness all their own, and Mr Sarne was no exception. We heard him tell us the old chestnut about young people creating the modern market because of the money they have to spend as though he had made a personal discovery. And as if the middle-aged didn't spend like water too anyway!

'The Choreography of Norman Morrice' was wholly satisfactory from the moment we were introduced into his studio until the first rehearsal of his new ballet faded out. Very wisely Morrice's commentary was recorded over a silent sequence. This is an infinitely more satisfactory device for all interviewees except the most assured and exhibitionistic than speaking to camera or to interviewer, although like television studio backgrounds it threatens to become a cliché (why is television such a Moloch of good, new ideas?) Morrice's personality is not of the Zeffirelli dominant kind; as he himself said, 'I'm not good at talking, writing, painting — movement is the only way that I think I can communicate'. Yet the pre-recorded talk flowed beautifully and naturally, while he was seen as naturally demonstrating the model scene, listening to the second-hand record bought in a Notting Hill market which inspired his ballet, demonstrating to his two dancers, finally receiving his inspiration back in their interpretation — and all this worked surely because he was not burdened with words or with a sense of the camera demanding any intellectual response from him. In fact at a certain moment the sound came direct, but the transition which must have been painless for him as it was painless for the viewer. So released from self-consciousness, Morrice, the rare creator who is not also a showman, gave as full account of his creative process as any man I have heard. I am not addicted to ballet but I found his explanation (so exactly synchronised visually) all absorbing. For a balletomane it must surely have been *Tempo*'s highlight.

Segovia . . . *'the fruit of endless practice'*

A little Mozart. Yehudi Menuhin at home — in the studio

'Mods and Rockers'

'*No good at talking . . . movement is the only way I can think. . . .*'
John Chessworth and Gillian Martlew in 'The Art of Norman Morrice'

I have discussed *Tempo* programmes dealing with the arts that require interpretation so that television's task is mainly to interpret the interpreter. As a writer I am impatient to come to *Tempo*'s treatment of literary themes, but before doing so, I must write a word upon painting and television. The memorable *Tempo* programmes that relate to painting appear to be few. This does not surprise me. Painters in action (save no doubt for Action painters) must be rigged to create a coherent programme. Great paintings of the past can only be dealt with in a more or less complex version of a lecture. This can be supremely effective as we all know from Sir Kenneth Clark's television talks on Michelangelo. But then Sir Kenneth is, in my opinion, the most incisive television personality we possess. The cameras helped him, of course, but television technique played a subordinate role. The only comparable programme on *Tempo* was 'The Face of Christ' — an analysis of the representation of Christ in art. Here I thought the camera technique — fading in and out from one painting to another — was a deterrent to appreciation, nor can C. Day Lewis as a narrator rival Kenneth Clark. But the programme will remain remarkable, for the script — intricate and powerful, although I disagree with its anti-romantic view — was written by the late John Whiting; as such it is in itself a contribution to literature.

In interpreting literature *Tempo* producers have preferred poetry to prose. Many of their poetry programmes have been effective and one, at least, was outstanding. Nevertheless it was in their treatment of Chekhov's short story 'The Dream' that the *Tempo* team produced one of their most original and successful pieces of television. As a prose writer I am no doubt biased. Nevertheless I shall pause for a moment to question this preference for poetry, especially since it is generally to be found in most television programmes on the arts. It lies deep, surely,

*And yet the man
    smelled of sweat'*

John Whiting's
view of Christ
Narrator — C. Day Lewis

in the make-up of television personnel. As a whole they belong to the
worlds of journalism, design, theatre or cinema; their instincts are
dramatic, visual, and even when they are most apparently concerned
with documentary realism, romantic; like people of the theatre and the
cinema, they are highly intelligent rather than intellectual and intuitive, practical rather than rational and ruminative; with a journa-
list's flair for the new, their artistic snobberies slant towards the contemporary or avant garde rather than towards the masterpieces of the
past; they are as distrustful of the academic as they are of the dowdy
(but not by any means so suspicious of the folksy as they should be —
especially if it be 'continental' or celtic folksiness). From this very
combination of qualities come most of the virtues of their work — style,
a sense of movement and form, a lively speed, great sensitivity to over-
tones of emotion, avoidance of the sin of dryness (with a propensity to
the far less grave sin of vulgarity), freshness and originality; but, of
course, such an approach has its deficiencies — arts programmes on
television (*Tempo* is no exception) lack intellectual toughness, any
acceptance of difficulty as a part of good art; their intellectual comment is sometimes pompous and pretentious; they fall too easily for
the 'arty' provided it can be tricked out to please the senses. Art,
perhaps, is made to seem a little uplifting and beautiful, and a little too
lightweight. A strong intermixture of the conflicting, the complex and
the solid would be my recipe for a new lease of life for television programmes on the arts, although I am well aware that the difficulties of
relating such qualities to pleasing and entertaining vision and sound
are considerable. But definitely a little more prose and a little less
poetry (if poetry means as it usually does romantic ballads or lyrics)
would save television art programmes from death by loss of weight.
However, that said, let me salute the programme 'Morning at Alamein',

an anthology of poetry from the desert campaigns. We come in through a staff-room chart on which is traced the forthcoming attack 'Scorpion', and through the chart we open on to a Scorpion tank, and with it move to our desert scene. Here around the tank are grouped its crew by whom or over whose actions the poems are recited. It is not always the case that actors prove good in near-static recitation; they seem too often to be deprived of their essential dimension of movement. Most of the actors in 'Morning at Alamein' seemed as though born to recitation. Grouped around their tank at their various duties, or awaiting the dawn battle, sleeping or writing letters, or merely (how ghastly is 'merely' here) staring before them, they delivered the poems without a trace of the voice beautiful, nor did they destroy all the rhythms as though they were under orders to disguise the poetry as prose. In fact the bitter, sad and humble mood of the soldiers' poetry that they gave us came over completely. Death as a greedy, though cunning, reaper was in every poet's mind. 'Do not think to provoke any immediate answer from death'. 'It is the harvest time in no man's land' — always Death's mouth about to devour sooner or later. If I were to criticise the actors' performance at all, it would be only to wonder whether the profusion of regional accents was not a somewhat distracting, irrelevant carry-over from sound radio, where they are so much needed for purposes of identification.

As the time came up to dawn and then to the advance the suspense created despite the counterpull of a static set was quite admirable. The mood of fear borne well and regret for life — 'I hate that dark and I love the light', 'We're not much . . . afraid', 'I'm not afraid but me and mine are hard to part' — was conveyed despite all the strain imposed on actors' facial repertory by the demands of close-ups. The battle din, though effective, was at times too much for the poetry (I doubt if such realism has any place in a programme of this kind). Most effective was the theatrical silence of the desert as the battle died away and the camera moved now on to one silhouetted corpse, now on to another — from an arm trickling with blood and on until at last it rested upon the dead man's head, face downwards, with his hair blowing in the dust-filled desert wind. 'He died the lad with a bruise — his bruise not to be mended'; 'their stillness is our comfort'. It was simple, romantic poetry, often Kiplingesque ballad in form. It seldom echoed the more famous poetry of the First War, except in its assumption that the best would be taken and the worse left behind. It was largely without the bitterness of Sassoon or Osbert Sitwell, though once the second-war poets questioned, 'The old usurpers reap what they cannot sow, will it be so again?' It was none of it poetry of the highest class; sincerity was its greatest virtue. But the television producers never let it down.

Three other programmes of poetry need mention, if only because they all began from the same general idea of national or regional poetry and each achieved such different effects.

I hope that the number of English viewers of 'A Grey Eye Weeping', a programme for St Patrick's day, was well above average. It will have done them good. When I was at school, hearty boys began their sentences.... 'You can always tell a stinker....' Well, you can always tell an English stinker if he is not utterly ashamed of our past record in Ireland; and this, despite all the clever excuses that can be found for us, not the least of which is the extreme tiresomeness of the Irish themselves. 'A Grey Eye Weeping' consisted of a series of the most bitter Irish poems, songs, and speeches (particularly impressive was Robert Emmett's speech from the dock in 1798) spoken by actors and a fine actress Eithne Dunne in the simplest Irish costumes. The camera moved from figure to figure as they stood or sat among various props

'Morning at Alamein . . .'

t is the harvest time in no man's land'

that well (though hardly as well as the real thing) suggested a bleak, bare, celtic-crossed Irish scenery. 'Royal Cashel is bare of house and guest' suggested the mood of the programme, but it whipped itself into a less austere, more frightening lament with the girl's greeting of her maimed lover returned from the English wars — 'Johnnie, I hardly knew you'. Perhaps it was the academic in me that wondered whether viewers could follow the rather complicated move from one historical period to another; perhaps, in fact, it doesn't matter if they didn't. At any rate it was a nice change from television's usual tendency to dot every i and cross every t at least three times.

There is no space in this book to describe in detail 'The Saltire in the Wind', a St Andrew's day offering when Glasgow and (blasphemy of blasphemies) Edinburgh were given the works in alternate lyrical prose and harsh invective. The programme must have knocked a lot of the surplus smugness out of Auld Reekie's God-fearing burghers. I can also only mention an anthology of Australian poetry, painting and prose — *They're a Weird Mob* designed to show that Ned Kelly isn't all of Australia, that Australian art is now not just down under but international. All these programmes showed satisfactorily, I think, that a common television prejudice against actors is completely unjustified. The actors' faces were always relevant, and a great deal more satisfying than voices over any montage of stills. One point, I must notice, about the Australian programme — the reading from Patrick White's novel *Riders in the Chariot* was the most effective recitation in the programme, yet the extract comes from a close-packed, long novel and does not even relate to Australia. There was no preliminary explanation of the plot or the character, and none seemed to be needed. So much for the belief that extracts from novels need too much filling in of background to be good television.

The Dream'

But, as I have said, the real triumph came in the reconstruction of Chekhov's story *The Dream*. The programme 'Two Tales for Christmas' attempted two different approaches to presenting short stories on the screen. The first was a short story especially written and read by Gwyn Thomas. It says nothing against Mr Thomas's work, though something, I fear, against his rather wooden narration, that the first story failed. It seems to me unlikely that any writer (or even actor) would have the dramatic power necessary to recite a whole short story to camera without leaving the viewers cold and dazed behind him. The powerful impression made by *The Dream* may have gained a little from following this failure in narration.

As Chekhov is conveniently dead, camera could take over from writer in narrating this story of an old pawnbroker's man alone in his shop on Christmas Eve. The place is full of the pledges of the poor anxious to find a little ready cash to provide some small addition to their dinner table on Christmas Day. Beautifully the camera tracked round them; in the half-light of the shop's dim mysterious recesses, they seem blurred shadows, indistinct forms that might perhaps prove to be no more than rags and lumber. And so they are or little more — these dresses and bonnets, bits of finery, jewellery, watches, clocks, a guitar. At the centre of the room the pawnbroker, played beautifully by Paul Rogers, sits in an old fur-trimmed coat huddled over the fire. Even when he lies down full length to sleep he seems — so clever is the camera work — no more than a shadowy outline whose eyes, or wrinkled cheeks, or grubby beard, or fleshy nose are lit up from moment to moment — highlights in a shadowy bundle not so different from the strange shapes of the pledges that hang from the beams of the roof. Every article seems to speak of that hopeless slum world of Moscow or St Petersburg — a world of venial debauchery, sorrow and crime — the world of the Marmeladovs or of Dostoevsky's poor folk. There seems something evil about the pawnbroker — perhaps it is the association with *Crime and Punishment*, or more probably that the sinister Dickensian bloom so apparent always in the urban poverty of nineteenth-century Russia, especially at Christmas time, is heightened by the touch of Fagin that Paul Rogers' make-up lends to the scene. Or is it, especially when he pores over the jewels, in his old fur-trimmed cloak that he recalls Volpone?

However the evil seeps into the scene, it seems almost tangible as the shadows and frost shapes appear like faces at the window of the close, stuffy room. We are with the frightening side of Hans Andersen. Fear is communicated to the pawnbroker... He turns and tosses. I have not seen a bad conscience so visually extended as to gather to itself every half-seen, half-heard thing in the room. Then, woken from his half-slumber by a terrible knocking, the pawnbroker takes a new shape — not as the master, the Fagin of his bullied, hungry little world, but as the squalid, rather pitiful instrument of oppression. The voice of his master tells him that he shall not go to Christmas morning mass, because there will still be hungry wretches ready to pledge their last pathetic possession for a little share of Christmas good cheer. I use a Dickensian vocabulary deliberately, for it is in Chekhov's short stories (his petty clerks and straining seamstresses) that via Dostoevsky the whole Christmas world of Dickens (and of Hans Andersen) finds its last respectable resting-place.

As the pawnbroker whom we now know not only as an instrument, but as an unwilling one, for he has come to his trade through necessity, the same necessity that drives his wretched victims to him, pauses in contemplation of his master's harsh orders, the silent world of the shop is pierced by the sudden reverberating note of a string that snaps on the guitar. It is a moment of alarm for him and for us viewers. Still the faces seem to peer at the window. Nearby sounds a shot and a cry, but when the old man goes to the window to peer out, there is only an old woman's voice piteously whining through the howling wind of the snowstorm. 'Your honour . . . your honour. . . .' 'It's poverty'. Something in the old man breaks and he begins desperately to thrust all the pledged objects out to the old beggar . . . coats, petticoats, cloaks, all, even down to the guitar.

And then over his shuffling, bewildered old figure we hear his words, 'I was tried a month later. . . . What for? . . . . I told the judges it was a dream. . . . You can't be tried for a nightmare. . . . But the court took my dream for reality'.

This surely is how prose fiction is to be conveyed on television. No stage performance could separate the thoughts and words from the scene as television can, no stage performance could reduce the central figure to a shadow and some sudden highlit grotesque features; no stage performance could give us the suggested faces at the window; no stage performance could assemble the whole story bit by bit as the camera passes from object to object. The cinema could — but what sense could there be in cinema so confining itself in space and in duration. In *The Dream, Tempo* took the words, the images from a printed book and brought them to life by purely television technique, as only the imagination of the most subtle reader of Chekhov's great short story could ever hope to do.

You can't be tried for a nightmare'
Paul Rogers in Chekhov's short story

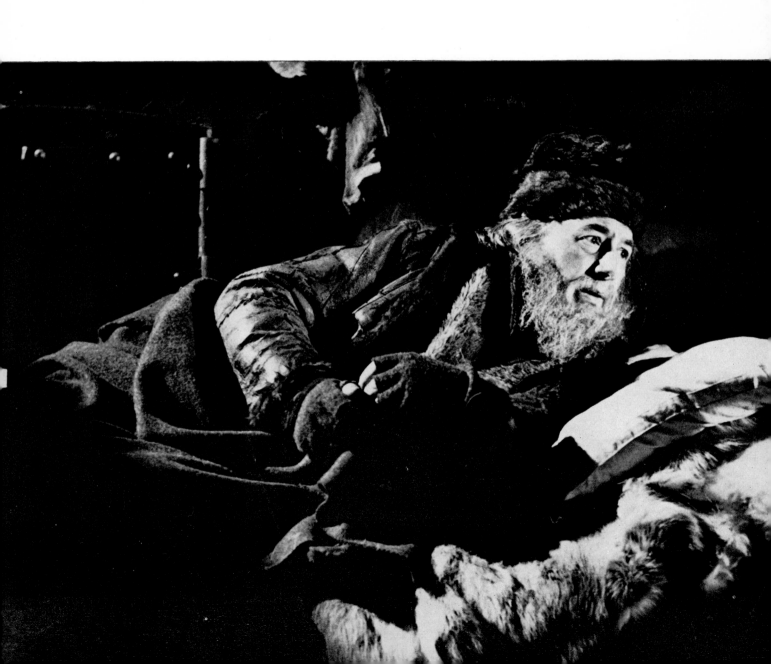

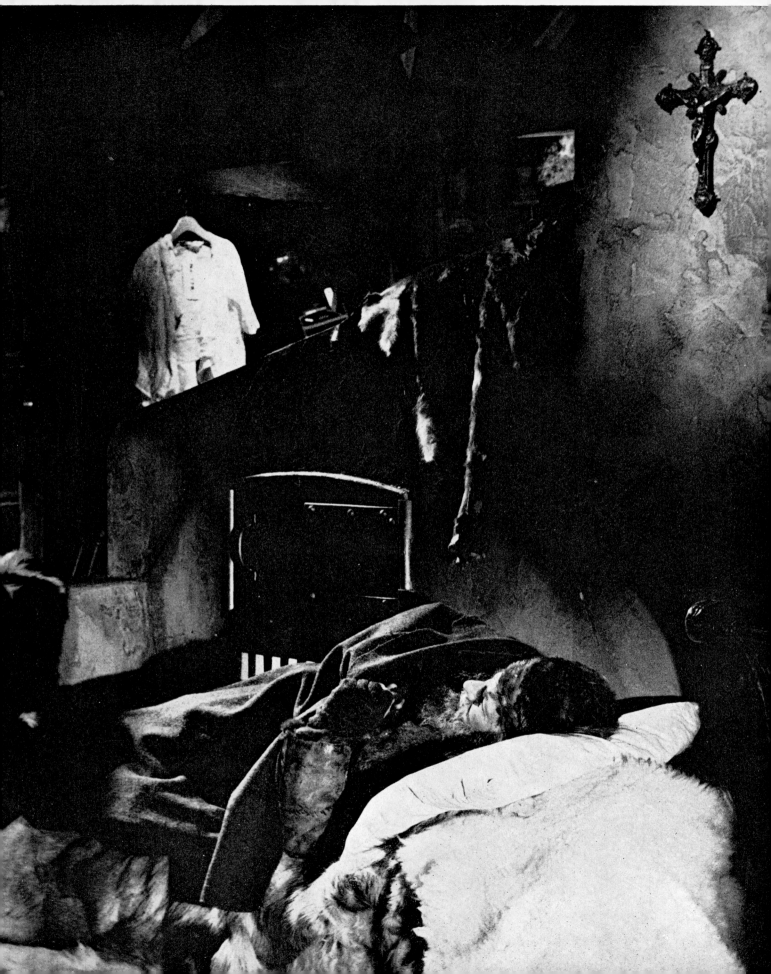

'Most things a man can do I'm up to . . .'
Two of the 'Weird Mob'

Hell fire from the pulpit . . .
Andrew Crawford in 'Saltire in the Wind'
A programme for St Andrew's Day

A Midsummer Madness
From 'Wooings and Weddings' —
A warning to June Brides

'*Royal Cashel is bare of house and gues*
Eithne Dunne in 'A Grey Eye Weeping
A programme for St Patrick's Da

Memories of Maxim Gorki
Baroness Budberg talks to Lord Harewood

he young Gorki

Gorki with the saint and the devil

Gorki and Stalin

orki and Tolstoi

Peter Sellers as the bad Scottish poet
McGonagall
'*A cow is much nobler
standing in the rain*'